GW01605388

The Business of Me!

Jamil R. El Bahou

Dear Will,

Enjoy the Book!

Best,

J.R. Bahou

Published by JR Bahou Limited

Printed by Book Empire, Leeds, UK
First Edition Print April 2019
ISBN 978-1-9160735-0-0

CONTENTS

PROLOGUE

PROLOGUE

When I decided to write this book, I wanted to share my story, and the story of our company. I also wanted to provide inspiration for our youngest leaders, young entrepreneurs, and anybody out there with the drive to succeed in business.

Much change is taking place in our industry, and while I and our organization undertake transformational steps to put us on the right footing for the next 10 years, I decided to share along the way my challenges, my hopes, and just a small piece of practical advice where I feel it most useful, relevant and important to any evolving business mind.

Through all of my trials and tribulations, and whilst this book is just the first chapter in what I fervently hope to be a long and adventurous journey, none of this would have been possible or achievable without the love, support and dedication of my family, and every person in our organization who continues to help drive our collective destiny forward.

To my father, who inspired me and taught me about honesty and perseverance. To my wife, Rana, who drove me and supported me from day one; and to my children, who give me the reason to wake up every day and reach for greatness.

I hope you all find this book useful and enjoy 'The Business of Me!'

Jamil R. El Bahou

THE BEGINNING

THE BEGINNING

Throughout this book, you will see repeatedly a strong emphasis on starting early. The seeds of success are sown long before the harvest.

I was born in the United States and moved with my family to Saudi Arabia when I was ten years old. Like most kids, I enjoyed a normal growing up period. In my latter teens, around sixteen or seventeen years old, I began to believe that if I wanted to succeed, I had to get ahead of the curve. Where that belief came from, I have no idea. I just knew that it was there.

After class, I would go to my father's office in Jeddah. My father had an Arabic education and he was my idol. It was natural for me to become interested in his work with his insurance business. I helped out around the office, writing the English correspondence, and picking up the rudiments of the business.

From my first year at University, I immersed myself in business books such as those by Richard Branson, and Jack Welch's, 'The GE Way'. Contrary to what my school friends were doing, I didn't waste my time.

I became motivated and dedicated to what I wanted to achieve.

When I graduated, I did not take a sabbatical like many of my friends. Instead, it made logical sense to me to head for Saudi Arabia where there was money to be made. I started working with my father in Jeddah a week after I graduated. I sold my car, gave away my dog, and became focused on the business.

The first thing I did was to set up a Business Development function for Dad's business. The old method was mostly by 'word of mouth', some of which, of course, still holds, but business seldom simply walks in the door and sits on your lap. At that time, just after the second Gulf War, business was difficult.

The expansion of the economy in Saudi Arabia was about to emerge. The period 2003 – 2013 was the right time to be in Saudi Arabia.

I introduced new clients and hired fresh graduates into the business. This was the beginning of my career.

A call from a client in Riyadh triggered a trip to the city. I was blown away by the place. It 'smelled of money in the air.' I felt, 'Something's gonna happen here.' I liked the US-style infrastructure of the place.

My father was reluctant about the idea of looking to do something in Riyadh, but I was convinced it was the place to be. I was not satisfied to accept to stay in place. We had to be in Riyadh.

I told my father that I would go to Riyadh, with no risk to him or the business. If I didn't make it, I wouldn't return. I was determined.

I arrived there with US$ 2,500 in my pocket and my laptop. I landed and sought out a convenient hotel to base myself. This was at the end of 2003. I found the Siteen Palace Hotel and got to work immediately among the neighborhood on my doorstep.

In a stationery store near the hotel, I purchased a printer and a business company directory. Most of the companies I wanted to visit initially were in the industrial area.

I went from door to door with these companies, asking to see the Finance Director in each of them, to talk to them about their insurance requirements.

I had arrived during Ramadan, and some of the companies worked later into the evenings.

One evening, I was taking a stroll near one of these companies and I walked in and simply asked the receptionist if I could arrange for a meeting with the Finance Director. The executive was in the office and agreed to see me right away.

So, here I was, a fresh graduate straight from university, walking into the Finance Director's office in a major company in Saudi Arabia pitching for his business. I was shocked that he was able to see me immediately like that. The timing was perfect, as my resources were running low.

The Finance Director was looking for advice on insurance, so my visit was at the 'right time, right place.'

I discovered he had also studied in Beirut. It transpired that he had met an uncle of mine, who apparently had been the only person to offer him a job at first when he newly graduated and was struggling to find a job. Guess what? He decided to sign me up on the spot. My first client.

What destiny!

There was enough in that initial contract to justify renting a small office, although I remained at the hotel, as the accommodation was reasonably priced and comfortable enough for me.

This was my first instance of an encounter with Fate.

In the next couple of years, we grew the business in Riyadh, and I began to think about the next step.

I was always fascinated by the world of Reinsurance. Everybody in the insurance business in the Middle East wanted to partner with someone from the London market, which was a great marketing tool in the marketplace.

The Bahou family had been in the Insurance business since the 1950s and 1960s and had done a lot of positive things for the industry locally.

I wanted and needed to do something to cement the family's legacy, something I had always thought about. I really had the desire to get the name established and respected at an international level. Lloyd's of London was the place to do that.

My advice to readers, and especially younger people who have a desire to succeed - start as early as you can. Create your destiny. Go for it. Don't wait for it to come to you.

Often, in discussions about my own career path, I advise people, "Don't be limited to your own backyard, your own locale, your own comfort zone. When you see a need or a gap, fill it before anyone else does. Lead the way."

Year after year, the number of people who break out, away from the pack, away from the herd, is falling as a percentage. They should start when they are younger.

The compiling, additive effect on the progression of your career gets better and better obviously the faster you are successful. Your income goes up, the satisfaction element increases. You get access to some of the so-called better things in life, the vacations, the car, the house. It is okay to relish these and enjoy them, but keep driving the progression, even when your income increases.

If fortune favors you, so be it, but don't sit back on initial success. As a young person, start immediately to work at your career and ambition. Begin the moment you start your working life. If you wait too long, time will take away the opportunities.

Your greatest work is available to you as early as possible. If you are young and fired up, ready to go, be creative of your own path. Blaze your own trail. Go for it!

The business world is a highly competitive place, and we live in the age of disruption.

Then along came Fate yet again, when I least expected it.

In early 2006, I was sitting at the hotel poolside, having a coffee when I learned that a small company in Bahrain with a Lloyd's broker accreditation was about to go out of business. The owner was looking to sell. The business was struggling and he wanted to exit. I met with him over a cheeseburger at Johnny Rockets, and took the decision to buy his company. We closed the deal on a handshake. This was in the Spring of 2006.

The company was called Crescent Global Insurance Services. It had only 4 or 5 employees. It had a negative Balance Sheet, and its License was about to expire within 90 days.

Persuasion is an art, a talent. Few people have it, to coherently build a picture, to sketch in your mind a scenario that will be accepted by others.

I have always believed I am a natural negotiator.

I flew to London to meet with the Lloyd's' principals there. I was only 25 years old at the time, and in hindsight I don't think they realized! They gave me the opportunity to present myself and my business vision to them. I told them I had taken over the company and we would be prepared to do what it took to become a value addition to the Lloyd's market as a Lloyd's broker specialized in our region.

To keep our accreditation, I would need to set up an office in London, hire staff, and demonstrate a need for Lloyd's markets for the business we handled. This, I duly did, and secured the continuation of the accreditation.

And so, I would acquire a place in the most conservative insurance market in the world. Being the ambitious person that I am, I accepted the challenge. Over the ensuing year, we established our presence in London and managed to funnel some business through the market, which permitted us to gain and keep our accreditation.

2006 was emphatically the most important year of my life.

The rest is history, from the small corps of staff in a tiny operation in Bahrain, Crescent Global Insurance expanded its presence to 13 different countries within a ten-year period. I want to pass on to you, readers, some of the many things which I learned along the way. If you are serious about making a success of yourself, and decide to read more, there are some things I would urge you to heed:

KEY TAKEAWAYS

1. Start early!
2. Be passionate!
3. Go for it!
4. Believe in Fate!
5. Whenever opportunity appears – grab it!

BUILDING THE BUSINESS

BUILDING THE BUSINESS

I have been asked many times, 'What is your secret? You have been able to accomplish so much in a short period of time – addressing culture, the economy, market forces, capital needs - what is your secret sauce?'

When an individual is perceived to be successful, one thing I have learned over the years is that 'perception is reality'.

In life, as in business, people want to be around successful people.

People want to do business with successful people.

People want to associate themselves with successful people.

Early on, I figured out quickly that presentation and substance are two of the most important things in building a business.

If you want to become a successful international business, you must grow like an international business.

You must act like a successful international business.

You must believe you are a successful international business.

The Basics:

An organization is like a human being.

Your brand has to be thought of as a human being. A positive, identifiable, living entity.

Create a behavioral style in the way you market and build a presence for your brand.

Be present where your market is present. Attend forums, meetings, industry panels, places where your clients interface with you and with the rest of your market. Be a recognizable force and a presence there.

Create proper, professional, well-presented brochures, logos, marketing and promotional material. Don't cut corners on this.

Define your vision and mission simply and repeatedly. Make it your mantra.

Have a platform to launch and to sustain your business.

Early, (again, early!), define what you want your organization, firm, company to be.

Tell it to all of your stakeholders, particularly your personnel, your teams who carry the banner. Embrace it wholeheartedly, no half-measures. Do it early, and keep doing it. This is key to the success of your business.

Substance and perception grow constantly, as does brand awareness, recognition, and reinforcement.

If there is no substance, what you have in your offering will be severely limited. It will not prosper in the longer run. It will have a limited competitive advantage, if any competitive advantage at all. Too many organizations fail because they simply drift along in their chosen markets.

Above all, you must be able to demonstrate measurable and tangible value in the products and services you offer.

Create a positive response to any client's question, 'Why choose Crescent to be an intrinsic part of my risk management?'

In the emerging markets where my business is located and operates, the Middle East, in the insurance world, we had to prove early (again) to our clients that we had something different to offer compared to the rest of the market.

'Why work with us?'

There's only one way to build a real business, and that's the hard way, no shortcuts, no favors, and no special treatment. To succeed, you need to be uncompromising, relentless, and neither accept free lunches nor give them out!

Every piece of business we ever had was done on the merits of tangible and demonstrable value.

In the beginning, as a small player, it was even more challenging. Every additional client was, and still is, precious. The growth of the portfolio becomes stronger with every single new piece of business that is booked. Even the smallest piece of business can be of value. That being said, new business isn't necessarily profitable business, so watch the numbers!

Time and place were implicit factors. Operating in

an emerging market is not the same as replicating the same thing in a more developed market. Opportunities would already have been recognized and acted upon in a developed market. Even with good people around you, it can be challenging.

Our target market at the time was the SMEs, the small and medium enterprises that constitute the backbone of the economy.

We began to establish our brand as well as our product and service range.

Then we hit the mattresses. It's the only proper way to grow your business.

Sell.

SELLING is a core building block of building a business, and it also happens to be an integral part of life.

Selling is like shaving. If you don't shave, like if you don't sell, you are a bum!

Sell we did! Every single client added to the next. A lot of little makes a lot. We applied the hard-selling push. And we sustain that selling push every day. In this way, we transformed from being a small operation to an international business with a presence in London.

Consider this thought: Most people think that their competition is next door. I cannot disagree more. My real competition is the person I look at in the mirror every morning.

Every day was a day that Crescent had to improve on what it did the day before, to compete constantly with itself.

When you think you are doing fine, you are at your most vulnerable. That is the time to re-commit to energizing your efforts every day again, pushing the limits all the time.

This is the way to success. Of course, sometimes force majeure steps in and there's nothing to be done about that except to manage your way through whatever crisis hits you and/or your business (see later references to the chapter on 'Crisis Management').

If you will always compete hardest against yourself, you are more likely to be successful, and more likely to stay successful. When a person or a company stops competing with themselves or itself, failure is not far behind.

The other form of competition has a way of expressing itself, that whilst you compete with others, those others will observe you. Never allow another person or company to shape your vision and mission. Only you can shape your own destiny.

KEY TAKEAWAYS

1. Be your own competition.
2. Build your brand.
3. Know what your company will be when you 'grow up'.
4. Refine your products and services to match what your customers really need.
5. Avoid the crowd – look for fresh markets.
6. Hit the mattresses.

CREDIBILITY AND ETHICS

CREDIBILITY AND ETHICS

We need a chapter on this subject because people tend to regard 'credibility' in a misconstrued manner.

People believe that a fancy CV, or a story of successes equates to credibility.

Credibility and success are linked, but credibility is something that permeates not only your business life, but also your private life.

Credibility is the total perception of other people of the trust in your business and in yourself. That what you say is what you mean, and that you will do what you say.

It doesn't always work out for the better. When you win, it doesn't necessarily mean that everyone wins.

Always commit to what you say you are going to do, whether it be to friends, family, or business partners.

People want to deal with people who keep their word.

Credibility doesn't mean that you always have to be good or take actions for the good. It means delivering on what you say you will do, regardless, so that people will believe you, and believe in you. They believe that you will do whatever it takes to follow through on what you say, even it means doing something against your own interests.

Keep in mind the old Latin saying, 'A man is a wolf to another man'.

On the issue of ethics, many will argue that being ethical is a highly subjective term, but if you start with your own moral compass, one option is to behave toward others as you would have them behave toward you.

In the real world, the perception of your ethics will be not only how and what you do, but also the consistency with which you do things.

Your ethical consistency should be part of your corporate and of your personal behavior.

Don't mix morality with ethics.

KEY TAKEAWAYS

1. Say what you do, and do what you say.

2. Always deliver, even at your own expense.

3. Morals are not ethics.

MANAGING SUCCESS

MANAGING SUCCESS

Financial success can sometimes be an Achilles Heel for a budding entrepreneur or an up and coming young businessman.

How can my success be an Achilles Heel?

How can my success be a negative?

I'm not your shrink. I'm not your girlfriend or your boyfriend. I'm just a guy writing a book. Everybody likes to dwell on their successes. We are human, and we have human reactions and sensitivities.

Many are in a hurry to buy that Rolex watch, to have that Ferrari, to own that nice house.

Of course, we seek financial success to be able to afford a better standard and quality of life for ourselves and our families, and there's nothing wrong with that in itself. However, it is imperative, regardless of how successful we are, that we should continue in the idiom of **WORK HARD, PLAY HARD, THEN WORK HARDER.**

Don't allow the financial successes to change the

resourceful and industrious person that you are, because that will ultimately be your professional downfall. I've seen it happen with so many people I've worked with over the years. A sense of entitlement is the worst thing that can happen to a budding entrepreneur or rising employee.

MARK MY WORDS, YOU ARE ENTITLED TO NOTHING BUT TO KEEP GOING LIKE YESTERDAY NEVER HAPPENED! NOBODY OWES YOU A LIVING, AND AS I HAVE SAID TO A NUMBER OF PEOPLE WHO ARE THANKFULLY NO LONGER AFFILIATED WITH MY ORGANIZATION, ESPECIALLY NOT ME!

Look at the title of this book, ***'The Business of Me!'*** I want to share with you some of my advice and experience on how to manage financial success.

LIVE THE MOMENT! And let it be the moment, but wake up every day as if you have nothing in your pocket and go out and work even harder than the day before.

Never wake up thinking, 'I'm too successful', or 'I'm too busy now, doing things other than grinding out each day's work.'

Don't compare yourself with other people you know, even friends that you know who have not yet reached the level of success that you have. These are false comparisons.

Don't ever be a successful sales guy who suddenly wants only to drive fancy cars and not go out and sell or to produce the intensity or the level of work as always. If you do that, your success will be short-lived, I promise you.

DON'T EVER BLOODY COUNT IT!

By all means have the cars and the bling and the 'stuff'. You deserve it, but don't ever let it distract you from being as hungry as you were in the first hour of the first day you started.

Avoid anyone who judges you on your status.

On the flip side, avoid people who want to cut you down because of your success. **REMEMBER THEY THINK THEY HATE THE PLAYER, BUT IT IS THE GAME THEY HATE BECAUSE THEY SIMPLY ARE NOT ABLE TO PLAY IT AS WELL AS YOU!**

KEY TAKEAWAYS

1. Don't dwell on your success
2. Wake up hungry every day
3. Enough is NEVER enough
4. Spoil Yourself, then get back to work!

INNOVATION

INNOVATION

The world, and everything in it is a moving target. Whatever holds constant today doesn't hold constant tomorrow.

If a business is not innovating, it is sinking, and sinking fast.

Innovation can mean a lot of things. Today, many think it merely refers to technological change as it relates to modern business. That is only one element of innovation, and an important one, but for this chapter, I want you to think about what YOU do every day. Examine constantly what your peers are doing. Be a student of your market. Of your industry, of your customs, of your local and regional economies, of your strategy.

Learn as much as you can as a constant practice.

Read, read, read.

Keep up to date.

As individuals who are business participants and industry players, it is imperative to recognize that we live in the age of platform revolution. And if you don't know what that means – look it up and learn!

Moving specifically to how innovation and technology is affecting our industry of insurance, those who don't figure out fast enough how to sell and interact with clients virtually, will be out of business before the decade is over. As I write this book, technology in our industry is gradually being brought into compliance and regulations. In other words, it is no longer than option!

Basically, Innovation is also differentiation, looking at everything we do as a business from start to finish, for you, for your clients, for all stakeholders.

Every step of the progression can be broken down and enhanced.

Break down things into little pieces to see if you can create economies of scale and efficiencies. Look at what you do similarly to your competitors, and look at what you do differently.

Look as well for inspiration in different aspects of your life. It is amazing what a walk in the park or on the beach will do for you when your brainstorming! I would also say the same for a good cigar and brandy, but that's for another time!

Just because nobody has done it before, it doesn't mean you can't invent it! Blaze your own Blue Ocean, and let others follow!

KEY TAKEAWAYS

1. The digital world is here to stay – get used to it.
2. Innovation needs to come from within - from within yourself – from within your own team – from within your own organization.
3. Break innovation down into pieces.
4. Innovation and differentiation provide competitive advantage.
5. Invent it if you must!

SECRECY and COMPETITIVE ADVANTAGE

SECRECY and COMPETITIVE ADVANTAGE

People cannot compete with you if they do not know what you are doing.

Your strategy needs to be a constantly moving target.

I never assume that all the people in the room are on the same page or tuned in.

It is amazing how much you can learn about your competition just by reading the press.

The more successful I am, the less I talk.

If you want to maintain your competitive edge, keep your core team small.

Split the secrecy/execution units into small pieces.

Keep up creativity, with no interruption.

Maintain a close cadre in your strategy team. Keep it compartmentalized. Each should only know what there is a need to know, relative to each unit.

Manage a hub and spoke operational system.

Starve the market grapevine of your news, until you are ready to invade!

Manage your messaging. PR and Communications is key to maintaining the public face of your organization. As we have learned recently, 'fake' news can be construed as real news, and controlling the message flow is as good as controlling the enemy 'propaganda' in time of war! **AND WHEN THEY ACCUSE YOU OF COLLUSION OR DISRUPTION IN WHATEVER FORM.... WELL...I WILL LEAVE IT TO YOU TO MAKE YOUR OWN ASSESSMENTS!**

Create superb execution skills.

Protect and manage the security of your cyber footprint. Document security is vitally important.

Invest in the best technology you can afford to protect it.

Ensure that people around you understand that everyone is working together as a team and should be aware of the dire consequences if the bond is broken or disrupted.

Loose talk kills businesses.

Walls have ears.

KEY TAKEAWAYS

1. Don't run your mouth.
2. Ensure your team doesn't run its mouth.
3. Invest in the best technology security.
4. Don't let lax computer controls leak your secrets.
5. You learn a lot about your competition from the Press.

PEOPLE and CULTURE

PEOPLE and CULTURE

It's amazing how many times companies hire directly from their competitors in the same industry. I never understood that philosophy for a single moment, unless you are trying to import processes or skills that you do not already have in-house, or don't have the capacity or ability to train to the skills level you need.

It is better to invest in fresh graduates and teach and train them to your standards and corporate mold.

Bringing in people from a competitor is sometimes the worst kind of poison you can introduce into your company.

Reshaping someone's mindset is difficult. I have always hired fresh minds and people and invested training time and effort and money in them. That way, the company preserves its unique identity and working idiom.

Many people complain about high turnover of staff or lack of loyalty. From my experience, the people you hire locally, home-bred, tend to produce less harm or disruption to your corporate culture.

At the start, if you are going to do it right, hire people with different ideas from people already within your industry, where people usually all think in the same way, the same patterns, the same rhythms. What we want is a cultural melting pot from disparate backgrounds. They could be lawyers, bankers, marketing executives from the retail sector, or even artists. They all have something to offer that's different. Fresh minds, fresh thoughts and ideas will stimulate the entire organization.

Your people are not just numbers, but many companies forget that. They are individuals, with their own dreams, hopes and families, the same as all of you reading this.

The key is to find harmony and a sense of common purpose from every person in your team, and in your organization. Otherwise, the people within your firm will not all pull in the same direction. Cohesion will just be a meaningless word in the dictionary.

People need to be treated fairly and firmly. While you should listen to your team's worries, hopes and aspirations, you should also be prepared to evaluate those who do not buy into the same level of commitment to their own future as that which they bring to your organization.

It is imperative for everyone's sake, and to build trust with your staff members to:

make it clear from the outset exactly what is expected from each individual staff member within their team and

let them know regularly what their contribution has been/ and is worth to the organization.

This makes the process of discussion about pay, benefits, bonuses and other compensation, so much easier and understandable for all parties.

Identify and be prepared to let go the bottom 10% of performers in your organization and regenerate. For HR Managers, I do not see this as simply the 10% who not do their jobs, but even more so for the 10% who do not fit into the organization and its directional thrust.

This latter 10% would be better off themselves in a different company if they do not fit into ours.

If the ship is leaking, sacrifice the few to save the many.

This is a decision that should be made not only in bad times, but also in good times.

Never be personal. From my experience, if you have had regular communication with, and have given honest feedback to your staff throughout the year about their performance, this should be an easy exercise.

Chief Executive Officers can unwittingly create prima donnas within the organization with appointments of people who know little or nothing about man-management and emotional intelligence. The fallout is never pretty. Do not give out something that you may have to take back later, especially if it is your own business.

If you are the owner, you are the only one who is taking the risk.

Always remember it is only a business. It is not your life. You must have the discipline to look at your business as if you are an outsider and to be able to make decisions such as downsizing or complete withdrawal if needed.

KEY TAKEAWAYS

1. Hire and train your own people.

2. Regularly let people know what is expected of them in their roles, and tell them how they are doing.

3. Don't recruit by putting your corporate hand into someone else's cookie jar.

4. Encourage misfits to leave for their own good.

5. Hire slow – fire fast.

NEGOTIATION

NEGOTIATION

If you are going to be a successful negotiator, to get what you want from a negotiation, from what TV channel to watch at home, to multi-million dollar deals, you must be patient. The more patient you are, the more likely you are to get what you want from the negotiation.

In order not to let the opportunities pass you by, have the patience to listen to the other side's demands before pulling the trigger from your side, **because many times, the strategy and position from the other side is actually more beneficial to you than your own starting position in the negotiation.**

Understand as much as you can. Let them show their hand before you show yours.

Being patient is worthwhile.

Don't be afraid to put your demands forward.

I've seen many negotiations fail, in love, life and business, because one of the parties could not put forward what they want.

Whatever you want, put it forward.

If you are not good at expressing yourself verbally, put it in writing, or get someone else to pitch for you.

IF YOU DON'T ASK, YOU DON'T GET!

Always know what your position is. Are you buying or selling?

If you are negotiating from a position of strength, take advantage of that.

If you are negotiating from a position of weakness, take what you can get.

Pick the right time, place and atmosphere for negotiation. There's no point to engage with the other side (be they business-counterparties, children, anyone) if they are not in a mindset to negotiate.

Don't offer to sell something if the other side is going through some crisis of their own.

Don't negotiate if there has been a leak of information from your side, as that will always be to your detriment. **SELL THE LOGIC! NOTHING BEATS THE POWER OF LOGIC!**

Negotiation is an art form, but not everyone is a negotiator.

Negotiation is the art of persuasion.

Sell your story. Create a story if you have to. Create a reasoning for your persuasion to convince the other side as to why and how they need to do the deal for their sake.

BE SINCERE! BE SINCERE!

Liars, con-men and bullshit merchants have very short careers as negotiators.

When dealing across other cultures, a deal is done only when the deal is done. Setting the tone is the most important factor when dealing with other cultures.

Do not re-negotiate what has already been negotiated UNLESS circumstances have changed for both parties and there is an appetite from both sides to get talking again.

YOUR WORD MUST BE YOUR BOND!

You are only as good as your handshake.

Without dwelling too deeply on the issue of legalities and contract law, good lawyers are worth their money. Have the best lawyers that you can afford and make sure they comply with international law.

Do your deals hoping for the best, but be prepared for the worst.

Make it clear at all times that you will enforce whatever the contract says. Ensure this is understood during the negotiations.

If you choose a particular legal jurisdiction, make sure there is an enforceable arbitration clause. Make sure your enforceability is cross-border.

Know your red lines—where your limits are before you will walk away.

KEY TAKEAWAYS

1. Don't be afraid to ask for what you want.
2. Be patient.
3. Draw your red lines and keep to them.
4. Make sure your agreements are enforceable.
5. Your word is your bond.

TIME MANAGEMENT

TIME MANAGEMENT

You have 24 hours in a day. To be truly successful you have to be prepared to work 48 hours a day!

All the comments about balancing work and life are the words of under-achievers.

Don't worry about life, it will take care of itself. I have seen too often, so many people with great potential under-achieving because they kept believing there was always tomorrow to do things instead of today.

Don't go home without finishing the day's mission.

If you have a deadline, work evenings, weekends, vacation time, whatever, to get it done!

If you don't, the only loser is you.

PERFORMANCE EQUALS OPPORTUNITY MINUS DISTRACTION.

It is not easy to be the poorest performer these days in any organization. Gone are the times when you could hide. Current performance management models have become more efficient.

Your job, your contribution, your performance, are all more readily measurable. So, why not stand and deliver?

If you have a true desire to get ahead in your career, work harder. There is no real substitute.

Channel your 48 hours' worth into the 24. Anything less is cheating only yourself and your own progress.

If you are not being rewarded for it, leave and find another organization which will value your contributions. There are many other companies out there which will welcome you.

If you desire to get ahead, and you can demonstrate that you can get more than a day's work in one day, you are better than most people in your own organization.

When managing your time, manage the elimination of distractions.

Beware the mumblers.

Beware the people who haven't done their homework before coming into your office.

Beware the people to whom you have to explain things five times over before they get it.

Time is your most expensive currency.

Prioritizing is the most vital thing in Time Management. Focus on the most important items.

Trial and error can get you through. Don't stop. Don't chase your tail, because you will never catch it.

KEY TAKEAWAYS

1. Get 48 hours out of each day.

2. Prioritize.

3. Recognize time is your most expensive currency.

4. Beware of mumblers and time-wasters.

PERSONAL VALUES/ BUSINESS VALUES

PERSONAL VALUES/BUSINESS VALUES

Do what's right.

Build your business the correct way or don't build it at all.

A business that will stand the test of time needs to be built on solid values and an honest foundation.

In this modern day, every business owner and employee is likely at some time to be offered short cuts to get ahead, some of which are immoral, and illegal.

There is no free lunch.

Be the guy with no skeletons in the closet.

As the owner and builder of a global business, I am always mindful to avoid situations or contentious areas where I may jeopardize the integrity of our brand and of our values.

The road is always longer for the virtuous, but the virtuous tend to stay that road longer.

When it comes to family, colleagues, and friends, always treat others as you want them to act toward you.

People ask me if I believe in karma – you bet your last dollar I do!

You reap what you sow.

As a budding businessman or entrepreneur, know the sanctions and financial crime regulations and laws in your market or markets.

KEY TAKEAWAYS

1. Do the right thing.
2. Do clean business.
3. Know your compliance regulations.
4. It is a marathon, not a sprint.
5. You reap what you sow.

STRATEGY and the ART OF WAR

STRATEGY and the ART OF WAR

Business is warfare!

It's not personal – it's business.

If you don't go to work every day to compete with yourself and with others with the ultimate purpose of coming home having made your company and yourself more prosperous, you should not be reading this book.

There's no morality in feeling sorry for the competition. To do so is fooling yourself.

Take the high ground always.

Attack your enemy while they sleep.

Don't fight the battle if you haven't won the war.

Plan your moves and purpose, and only execute when you are sure of success.

Everybody loses in a head to head fight.

Avoid direct confrontations if possible, but if you must

confront, try to draw your enemy's resources first. Let them expend their resources.

Strategy is more than simply business development plans.

To be a student of strategy is to be someone who knows the past, the present and the trends and movements within their industry and beyond.

Strategy is creativity.

Blaze your own path. Don't follow the industry.

Manage your financial resources because they are not infinite.

Competitors may not be your friends today, but they may very well be tomorrow. When you compete, compete with class and integrity. A competitor of yesterday, may be your client of today or tomorrow.

It *is not* personal – *it is* business.

You owe it to yourself and your company to go for the win every single time.

The only man who counts is the man left standing.

If you are not a student of war, become one.

You need to learn how to identify advantage and disadvantage; when you have the high ground; and when to attack and when to retreat.

If none of this interests you, close the book now and throw it away.

That being said, there is nothing wrong with forging strategic alliances to advance short-term strategies. I say 'short-term' strategies, because the words, 'long-term' and 'alliances' are conflicting in my view.

In this Age of Global Disruption, no strategic planning, no matter what it is, should exceed 18 - 24 months, and should be re-evaluated and re-validated every 6 months.

Cash is King – Cash Flow is everything.

When the competitive terrain is against you, don't expand. Too many people make the mistake of going hell for leather in good times. Such aggressive moves are foolish, and play into the syndrome of the Law of Diminishing Returns.

Invest when the market is down. Sell when it is high. This is common business sense.

Strategy is about going long and always knowing what the next move is worth to you.

I find it amazing that so many peers are trying to swim faster in a red ocean or in a settler industry.

If you are going to invest a million dollars, know what your returns are going to be before you do so.

Don't expand merely to get marginal returns.

Game, don't gamble. Know the difference.

On execution – plan, plan, plan.

In scenario development, don't focus on what you already know, or think you know, but tell me what it is that we don't know.

Try to figure out what we don't know, and be prepared to reinvent yourself and start over when necessary.

KEY TAKEAWAYS

1. Competitors are not your friends today, but may be so tomorrow.

2. Cash is King – cash flow is everything.

3. Plan, plan, plan.

4. If you are not a student of War, become one.

CRISIS MANAGEMENT

CRISIS MANAGEMENT

Shit happens! But what doesn't kill you makes you stronger.

Be prepared for it. Don't fear the unknown. Embrace it. Make it your friend.

The only things that really matter are your sanity, your health, and to remain focused and in control, which means principally in control of yourself.

Good deals go bad.

Sometimes you should have seen it coming. Other times it is a real surprise.

A crisis can be in the family or in the business. One thing I've learned, is that every problem or situation gets resolved, one way or another.

Learn from your mistakes. Move on and grow because of them.

Remember that some of the greatest business people in history have been bankrupt multiple times and still made comebacks, even to the top of the world stage.

A crisis is an opportunity to learn, so don't miss your chance.

Take in the gift of fearlessness as it comes along in your journey.

That being said, be prepared.

Spread your risk.

NEVER have all your eggs in one basket.

Your reaction to any crisis will depend on the peculiar nature of the crisis, and the resources at your disposal.

There are battles that you cannot win. The only thing that matters is to win the war, and striving throughout to keep moving forward.

Hold firmly to your values, ethics, morals and strategies.

The only thing that matters in a crisis is that you are left still standing, or in a position to pick yourself up.

I guarantee that in a real crisis, the only person you can truly count on is yourself.

Lay out for yourself what your options are and keep your cards close to your chest.

Be prepared to smoke others out of their foxholes, and when you do that, show no mercy. Go for the metaphorical kill.

KEY TAKEAWAYS

1. Don't panic.
2. Lay out your options.
3. Wait it out.
4. The only person you can rely on is yourself.
5. Feed off the gift of fearlessness.

The ART of WALKING AWAY

The ART of WALKING AWAY

Many people don't understand the term, **'Zero-Sum Game'.** I live by it.

Just like life, business is a mix of risk and reward. You risk your resources, your reputation and your future every day. Why not make it worthwhile?

When you are building a company from scratch, just as you build a name for yourself from scratch in any business or environment, it is important to get your name out there, even at a marginal profit to build that company or personal reputation.

However, once you have built your business and reputation, know your worth. Your time is your most valuable commodity. Putting the correct value on your time and your services will always yield better returns.

If you do not have enough time, you cannot take on other, better business.

Everything has its price, but it is up to you to accept or refuse that price. Walking away can be a tough decision, especially if you are walking away from something you really want. But remember this, bus schedules are there for a reason. If you miss one, you wait, there will be another one along before too long.

Example: You may be interested in buying a company. You do the due diligence. You check the numbers. You map out the economies of scale. You reckon the long-term value of the potential acquisition. You know what you should be paying. However, the numbers don't stack up. **WALK AWAY!**

Example: Sometimes business relationships are profitable to begin with, then become less so. If you cannot re-negotiate revised better terms. **WALK AWAY!**

KEY TAKEAWAYS

1. Don't break your own red lines.
2. Deals that look too good to be true are just that – too good to be true.
3. Listen to your numbers.
4. Don't fall in love with the deal.

The POWER of the NETWORK

The POWER of the NETWORK

We live and work in a world that has become truly globalized and it is vital to be able to trade effortlessly and seamlessly cross-border.

In 2013, I founded GBN –The World's Insurance Network, an ecosystem of the globe's leading insurance organizations.

In today's international markets, if you are unable to service the needs of your clients beyond your local borders, you have limited chance of growth and/or survival.

It is a small world out there, and the ability to start business, exchange ideas, and pool resources with like-minded organizations creates incredible synergies. It expands not only one's own horizon and network, but also those of all the other counterparties involved.

Networks in general are a great tool, not only for business at large, but for anyone wanting to build their relationships, their careers, and their own businesses.

Perfecting the art of networking is perfecting the art of building and maintaining an ever-flowing pipeline of opportunities.

SO, GET OUT THERE!

In six short years, the GBN family has grown from a membership base of 40 of us to over 140 organizations, employing tens of thousands of people, together transacting billions of dollars' worth of insurance premiums per annum.

If you are in the insurance industry, compare your own organization, and ask yourself, 'If I am not part of a network, what potential do I really have if I remain solo, out on my own?'

GBN is certainly not an easy club to get into, but there are others out there with slightly lower barriers you may wish to consider accessing.

KEY TAKEAWAYS

1. Network, network, network!
2. Put yourself out there.
3. Recognize the power of many.
4. Even though you are reading my book, and think you may want to join GBN, I would encourage you to approach us.

On BEING a SALESMAN

On BEING a SALESMAN

There are no short cuts in Sales.

If you are a salesman and you are reading my book, it probably means you have drive.

Selling is an art.

In order for that art to bear fruit, there's a couple of pieces of advice which I know worked for me, given my sales background.

Nobody wants to do business with a bum. If you are going to the extent of representing yourself or your business, whether you are male or female, clean up.

First impressions are everything.

I'm not going to tell you how to dress, because there are whole books about fashion.

Always aim to be in professional attire.

Professional sales people don't go to sales meetings in shorts or flip flops or with enough metal sticking out of them to set off 20 metal detectors.

Call me old-fashioned, but if you want to get ahead, you have to look the part.

You can never make enough sales in a day. The more people you call, the more you have the opportunity for more people to hear what you have to say.

When you get those meetings, keep it concise, get straight to the point, and practice your 30-second 'elevator pitch'.

Nobody likes a 'chatterbox'.

Going into a sales meeting, you have to be prepared to give a brief company background, what it is you're selling, and why the person on the other side will find it attractive.

If you don't value what you're selling, nobody else is likely to value it either.

Believe in it, and again, be prepared.

Do your homework.

Be respectful of the competition, another Rule of War.

Never bad-mouth your competition.

Maintain professional etiquette, such as 'thank you' calls, follow-up emails, and don't be pushy.

Leave the door open for future engagements.

You will win some, and you will lose some. Nobody likes a sore loser. Keep smiling, regardless.

Enjoy the game and you will win more often.

Never leave home without a business card in your wallet and, if you need it, a company brochure.

KEY TAKEAWAYS

1. There are no short cuts in Sales.
2. Always dress in professional attire.
3. Practice your 30-second 'elevator pitch'.
4. Do your homework.

LAW and ORDER

LAW and ORDER

I talked earlier about having the best lawyers. Double down on that investment.

Whilst most people go into contractual arrangements in good faith, things can go wrong, especially when the good faith does not end up being reciprocal.

Always read the fine print.

Take the best legal advice you can afford.

Choose your law and your jurisdiction.

Many people make the mistake of drafting hastily made Memorandums of Understanding or Agreements, thinking they are legally binding. Guess what? Most of them are not.

Different countries have different legal systems, and it is of the utmost critical importance that you put the context of the legal agreement within the jurisdiction in which it is meant to be enforced.

Get smart on arbitration – it will save you a fortune.

Moreover, understand the time frame for potential litigation and the cost of any litigation before you put it in motion.

Sometimes the cost of enforcement and litigation is more than it is worth.

Under no circumstances do a deal whose conditions you cannot enforce.

Even more relevant and important, is to advise the other party that it would be in the best interests of a harmonious agreement that they should obtain their own separate legal advice in relation to contracts under consideration, so that they completely understand the consequences of not sticking with the terms of the contract.

Never sign a contract in a language you don't understand.

KEY TAKEAWAYS

1. Choose your law and jurisdiction.
2. Hire the best lawyers you can afford.
3. Understand the language in contracts.

BEING YOUR OWN BOSS

BEING YOUR OWN BOSS

I am frequently asked, 'What is it like working for yourself?'

It is bloody hard!

There are perks of course. I work when, where and with whom I choose.

But it is not all fun and games. Working for yourself means the ultimate responsibility for your success or failure depends on you. The buck really does stop at your desk.

That is not a responsibility or pressure that everyone is able to carry, and that is just fine. Every one of us has a role to play in keeping the world and society moving, otherwise it would be chaos.

One thing I will say about being my own boss is that there is no 'I' in the word, 'team', and I have been able to be my own boss and to continue to do what I do day by day because I have been fortunate to be surrounded by some of the brightest and best people I know.

People working together with a common vision, mission and sense of purpose is what makes good companies become great companies.

As the Commander-in-Chief of any organization, it is not always the easiest job to keep people focused on the mission. Sometimes the pressure to deliver is excruciating.

In my view, leading from the front demonstrates absolute commitment from the top to drive the team forward. Doing it this way, everyone involved gets to a better place.

I'm not going to pretend it is a democracy, but being your own boss, 'It's my way, or the highway – for better or for worse, until Death you and your business part –Amen!'

KEY TAKEAWAYS

1. Being your own boss is bloody hard!
2. The buck stops at your desk.
3. There's no 'I' in 'team'.
4. It's not a democracy - it's my way, or the highway.

CONNECTING the FUTURE -the VIEW from the TOP

CONNECTING the FUTURE -the VIEW from the TOP

One of the most regular questions I am asked is about how I see the future. Where do I see the industry, the country, the region, and the world, going?

As a business leader, I undoubtedly have access to information at unique levels. In the boardrooms and executive suites there are things visible, not usually seen from lower positions – The View from the Top.

It is a complicated world that we live in. Putting together all the smaller pieces of the jigsaw or mosaic to see the broader picture is a useful exercise. Even then, it is difficult to predict what happens next.

We live and operate in the Age of Hyper-Disruption, where constants and facts normally held true are altered in an instant without warning, with a global landscape moving in parallel.

For many of those involved in our insurance industry over the past 20 years, scenarios have been relatively constant and predictable. Although we saw the greatest amount of capital influx during that 20-year period, plus the faster development of the emerging markets, that period is now at an end.

Depending on where you are in the world, and every market has its own idiosyncrasies, opportunities, circumstances and challenges, the next 5 to 10 years will likely leave our industry changed forever, particularly from a London market perspective.

To connect the future, you must be able to be nimble, creative, dynamic, digital, and cross-border.

You need to be able to shift resources, break down cost centers over various geographies, and be vertically integrated.

In a market with diminishing returns, trying to reinvent itself, and by this, I mean Lloyd's and the London market, change is demanded all the way along the production chain.

Underwriting, placement, and processing must be eliminated. The only way to do that is to be digital.

We need to recognize that the Age of Digital and the

Internet of Things is upon us with a vengeance.

A new economic order built around cyberspace is the business reality of today.

It is happening not only in our insurance industry, but it has also already happened or is happening right now everywhere.

Get involved.

Get smart and dive right in, because if you or your organization lack the ability and capability to trade in cyberspace, you will be out of business even before I write my next book.

Digital is sweeping the industry like a tsunami that hits without warning.

What this means is that with time, the people market which has existed for hundreds of years, will cease to exist in our industry in the form we know it.

Two years ago, I stood up in our London office in a room full of traditional, hard-edged, London brokers who worked for me at the time, and said, 'We wanna be a Google. We don't wanna be an AON. Those who wanna work for a Google, stay with me. Those who wanna work for an AON, there's the door.'

It was the best thing I had said all year.

We had been working secretly on the Connect Project for a full two years up until that time, and at that moment, the Connect Project was truly born.

We just managed to begin transforming our team and our way of doing business right in time before the market tsunami struck.

Shortly thereafter, Lloyd's mandated electronic standards for all Lloyd's managing agents. All the Lloyd's brokers were given an ultimatum to begin going digital by June 2019, or face the consequences. By that date, every Lloyd's broker had to be signed up with a Lloyd's-recognized electronic placement system.

The insurance industry arms race had begun, and we already had an arsenal.

As of this writing, we are working tirelessly with the market and our peers to move the industry forward.

We made a strategic decision to become an open platform for all, and offered our technology to the market. That includes Lloyd's managing agents, company markets, coverholders, and Lloyd's brokers, essentially transforming us from a market player to the operator of a market wide next generation electronic platform for all.

In January, 2019, Lloyd's approved our Connect Marketplace gateway platform as a Lloyd's recognized electronic processing system.

As I write this, the next phase of what I hope to be an incredible journey and chapter in my life has begun....

KEY TAKEAWAYS

1. The insurance industry is about to change radically forever.

2. Whether or not you are in insurance, observe how technology is impacting your industry.

3. The books on Business Theory will be re-written several times over the next two generations.

LIVING, LOVING and LEAVING a LEGACY

LIVING, LOVING and LEAVING a LEGACY

In life, it cannot all be about work, and it cannot just be about business. You need to keep a balance. Life is short.

Many people go through life without purpose, with no sense of self-perception about the meaning of their own existence.

Most people come and go without leaving any trace. It is okay to be one of those people.

For me, it is about living, loving, and leaving a legacy.

Take advantage of whatever you have.

Be a positive influence on your family, friends, co-workers and your community.

Serve your country if you have the opportunity to do so.

Remember, especially if you have kids, that your country competes just like you do on a daily basis and needs all the patriotism it can get to make sure it remains competitive and a worthwhile place to live in for future generations.

Drop the sense of entitlement, you don't have one! None of us have it.

Leave something behind as a legacy.

Most people will not have the chance to leave their mark on anything in this world.

Legacy itself does not necessarily mean putting your name in the history books, or a stamp in your community.

Legacy means raising a family, inspiring others to over-achieve and doing something to be remembered by.

On the question of love, start by loving yourself, because if you cannot love yourself, you cannot love others.

Love is the most precious of all commodities and source of pride that a human being can hope to have.

Love drives you forward.

Love for your family.

Love for your work.

Love for your country.

Love creates.

Love builds.

Love delivers the life of happiness we all desire.

It is love that drives you to do the greatest things you will ever do in your life.

Living is experiencing. The more you experience, the more you live.

NOW GO OUT AND PURSUE THE BUSINESS OF BEING <u>YOU!</u>

MARRIED to SUCCESS
by MRS RANA El BAHOU

MARRIED to SUCCESS
by MRS RANA El BAHOU

A lot of women ask me, "What is it like to be married to success? What is it like to be married to someone always on the go, somebody so driven, somebody who never switches off, and somebody so busy?"

My answer is, "It is never easy. Basically, as a woman, our goals are different from those of our partner. Whether it is to raise a family, or keeping a household together, supporting your partner, developing your own career, if that's what you wish, or simply pursuing your own personal interests. But, you also have to be a team."

Being married to success is not easy. For those women reading this who have already experienced this, you will understand where I'm coming from.

One thing about being married to a successful businessman is the changed pace of life. Parties, conferences, conventions, business trips, and the 'don't leave home without it' syndrome.

You may be married to the boss, but he is still your other half. Protecting your husband's interests means keeping a balance.

It is not all about sunshine and beaches. Sometimes it does rain. Your partner, being the successful leader of industry that he is, has his downs as well as his ups.

The Devil Does Wear Prada! If there's anything a woman wants, it's what she can't have. Guard your man like a hawk, ladies, because the game is on.

One thing I do know, I am keeping an eye on this one!